Rebekah Pearse

Text copyright © 2011 by Rebekah Pearse.
Photographs copyright © 2011 by Ara Shimoon & Rebekah Pearse.

All rights reserved. No part of this book may be reproduced in any form without written permission from the publisher.

SWEET
Seasonal Desserts

REBEKAH PEARSE

PHOTOGRAPHS BY
ARA SHIMOON & REBEKAH PEARSE

for Nectar

offered me some tea.
sent for me one of t
d in the fluted val
g morrow, I raised t
mixed with the cru
was happening to m
And at once the vic
n having had on me th
mediocre, contingent,
the tea and the cake
it mean? How could I

Contents

SOME THOUGHTS ON DESSERTS

WINTER
Single Malt Scotch Ice Cream — p.21
Blood Orange & Buttermilk Tart — p.22
Hazelnut Baci — p.25
Keegan's Spiced Pecans — p.27
Sweet Potato Pecan Tart — p.28
Walnut & Rosemary Caramel Tart — p.31
Honey Tangerine Sorbet — p.32
Carrot Chiffon Cake — p.34
    w\ Maple Frosting — p.37
Fleur-de-Sel Caramel Ice Cream — p.40

SPRING
Punk Rock Rhubarb Fool — p.45
Passionfruit and Mango Tart — p.46
Fromage Blanc Cheesecake — p.49
Lemon Lavender Shortbread — p.50
Buttermilk Ice Cream — p.53
Fragrant Lemon Tart — p.54
Rum & Raisin Roundies — p.57
Lemon Berry Chiffon Cake — p.58
    w\Lemon Frosting — p.61
    & Lemon Mousse — p.62

SUMMER

Honey Ice Cream	p.69
Blackberry & Passionfruit Mousse Tart	p.70
Peach Cobbler	p.72
Berry Conserve	p.75
Key Lime & Blueberry Tart	p.76
Summer Berry Sorbet	p.79
Cherry Cheesecake Tart	p.80
Triple Raspberry Tart	p.83
Fig & Honey Mousse Tart	p.84
Blue Cheese Ice Cream	p.86

HARVEST

Apple Pudding Cake	p.91
Sweet Corn Ice Cream	p.92
Sour Cherry Crumble Tart	p.95
Oatmeal Raisin Cookies	p.96
Damson Plum Compote	p.97
Roasted Apple & Chestnut Tart	p.99
Sticky Toffee Pudding	p.100
w\ Whisky Caramel Sauce	p.102
Pistachio Ice Cream	p.103
Sugar Pumpkin Cheesecake	p.105

HOLIDAYS

Gingerboys	p.111
Cranberry Cardamom Shortbread	p.112
Vanilla Bean Sugar Cookies	p.115
Newschool Fruitcake	p.117
Roasted Pumpkin Tart	p.120
Wild Cranberry Butter Tart	p.123
Eggnog Ice Cream	p.124
Ginger Ice Cream	p.125
Red Velvet Cake	p.127
w\ Vanilla Bean Frosting	p.129
Red Velvet Rum Balls	p.132

BASE RECIPES

Vanilla Tart Shells	p.135
\Chocolate Tart Shells	p.137
White Chocolate Mousse	p.138
Homemade Mascarpone	p.139
Vanilla Bean Syrup	p.140
Vanilla Bean Custard	p.142
Chantilly Cream	p.143
Candied Lemon Zest	p.145

SOURCES   p.146

INDEX   p.147

ne tea, a thing I did
e of those squat,
d valve of a scallop
ised to my lips a sp
e crumbs touched m
g to me. An exquisite
ie vicissitudes of
me the effect which
gent, mortal. Whe
e cake, but that it i
uld I seize and appre

SOME THOUGHTS ON DESSERTS

Dessert is special. Unlike other foods, we don't eat it just to satisfy hunger, we use it to treat ourselves, to mark important celebrations, to thank and to reward.

Sweetness, the only taste for which all humans are born with a natural preference, holds a place of honour in our culture.

Not only do we eat desserts on special occasions, we make it a point to share them, an act of intimacy and friendship.

From the cook's perspective, desserts offer an amazing opportunity for creativity, their very nature being playful. Experimentation can produce mind-blowing, charming, silly, sensuous or sophisticated (but ultimately delicious) results.

Unfortunately, desserts are often prepared from the poorest of ingredients. Because we are so predisposed to enjoy sweets, we stuff ourselves with low-quality fare designed to satisfy the sweet-tooth but not the soul.

We've come to perceive sweets as commonplace, a commodity, something to pick up on impulse while waiting in the grocery line. Vanilla, a product made from the stamen of a rare tropical orchid (and one of the most beautiful flavours in the world), has become a synonym for boring or everyday.

Worst of all, as a population, we're overweight and unhealthy, with a slough of health issues related to the amount of sugary garbage we shovel down our gullets every day.

What should we do?

First, we need to stop eating that stuff! We don't need to forgo it completely, but cut back. It's not good for us! The amount of additives, preservatives, stabilizers, resins, gums and chemicals in commercial sweets is unreal, not to mention the environmental and social impact of sweeteners made from corn.

Does that mean that sweets are bad?

Of course not! But if we're going to indulge, we can enjoy something made from real ingredients: real fruit, real butter, real cream and lemons! Not only will our taste buds thank us, but I firmly believe that we find it more *satisfying*.

Processed foods, and processed desserts in particular, simply do not satisfy. I'm convinced that the reason we shovel in such awful stuff is that our bodies don't recieve any satisfaction or benefit from low-quality foods, and continue sending us signals that we need to keep eating. What we fail to see is that we need *real* food, not more of the same.

Real food made with real ingredients scratches the physical and mental itch. It interacts with the body in such a way that you feel full, content and nourished after eating.

The desserts in this book are all made with real, nourishing, satisfying ingredients. More specifically, they're made with ingredients *in season*.

As a culture, we've lost track of where our food comes from and how it is grown. We go to the grocery store and see peaches in March and apples in July and we don't even bat an eye.

A crucial part of eating real food is being willing to eat with the seasons. There's nothing like the pleasure of biting into a ripe summer peach and feeling the juice dribble down your chin, just as there's no better taste in autumn than the fragrant crunch of a fresh-picked apple. Why would anyone want to eat a wooden peach in spring or a mealy apple in summer?

Find the closest farmer's market. Buy a jar of local honey, a pound of unsalted butter, and a basket of whatever fruit smells the best, then turn it into dessert. Don't feel guilty, enjoy it and share it.

Dessert is one of the best things life has to offer. Make sure you're doing it well!

WINTER

Long nights, brisk air and snow-filled fields cry out for the comforts and pleasures of dessert.

Without the bounty of fresh produce available the rest of the year, the dessert cook must turn to nuts and essences, spices and caramel.

Vegetables are required to do their duty in wintertime; the humble squash, carrot and lowly sweet potato are all coaxed into sharing their affinities for sweetness.

In olden days, oranges were treasured as a winter delicacy and to this day they are at their peak in the winter months. Their sweet perfume and fresh tang offer relief from the dearth of quality produce.

Liquor often plays a role as well: the warming that comes from a dram of scotch makes for an ice cream worth eating no matter how cold it is outside, its subtle flavours of caramel, spice and orange peel blending perfectly with the other tastes of winter.

SINGLE MALT SCOTCH ICE CREAM

Makes about 2 pints (1 litre) of ice cream

2/3 cup heavy cream

2/3 cup whole milk

8 egg yolks

1/3 cup granulated sugar

1 oz good single malt scotch

I call this one grown-up vanilla because of it goes so well with everything

Over medium heat in a heavy bottomed pot, warm the cream and milk together

In a separate bowl, whip the yolks and sugar together until smooth, fluffy and lightened in colour

Whisk the hot cream mixture into the yolks a bit at a time until they are warmed

Whisk the warm yolk mixture back into the remaining hot cream in the pot

Cook over medium heat, stirring constantly until the mixture coats the back of a wooden spoon

Pass through a fine mesh strainer into a bowl set in an ice bath to stop the cooking process immediately

Chill in the refrigerator at least 8 hours

Stir in the scotch right before spinning

Follow the instructions on your ice cream maker, removing the ice cream when it looks like a thick milkshake

Freeze at least 4 hours to allow the ice cream to set

I recommend a good Highland scotch for this recipe. The same rule applies to cooking scotch as cooking wine: you should be happy to drink it, but there's no need to break the bank. Additionally, I'd steer clear scotch from Islay. Its smokiness is better for pairing with chocolate than with ice cream

BLOOD ORANGE & BUTTERMILK TART
Enough for eight 4" tarts

1 ¾ cups granulated sugar

3 Tbsp room temperature unsalted butter

4 eggs

¼ cup all-purpose flour

1 ¼ cup full-fat buttermilk

6 Tbsp fresh-squeezed blood orange juice

¼ tsp Tahitian vanilla extract

8 chilled, unbaked tart shells (p.135)

When baked, this filling forms a thin crust, a thick, dense citrus layer and a creamy center. Arrange candied blood orange slices on top for a grand effect

Preheat the oven to 350F (165°C)

Place the butter and the sugar together in a mixing bowl and beat with the paddle attachment until fluffy and light in colour

Add the eggs one at a time, scraping down the sides of the bowl with each addition

Combine the buttermilk, blood orange juice and vanilla

Add the buttermilk to the egg mixture and beat until the sugar granules are dissolved (a hand blender works great for this)

Pour into the tart shells until ¾ full and bake 10 minutes, then turn and bake another 10 minutes until the filling has puffed up and started to brown slightly

Allow to cool before serving

Blood oranges typically show up in January. In addition to their beautiful bright red colour, they feature a particularly aromatic juice and zest

HAZELNUT BACI

Makes about 3 dozen cookies

Ingredients:
- 2 cups (270 g) whole hazelnuts, skin-on
- ¾ cup sifted icing sugar
- 1 ½ tsp freshly ground nutmeg
- 4 egg whites
- 36 whole hazelnuts, for garnish
- icing sugar

These cookies are naturally flourless, and the basic formula of ground nuts, egg and icing sugar works for any kind of nut. Play around!

Pre-heat the oven to 350F (165°C)

Toast the hazelnuts in the oven until the skins are dark brown and pull away from the nut meat

Dump the hot hazelnuts onto a clean towel and rub them between its layers to remove the charred skins

In the bowl of a food processor, grind the hazelnuts until they are the texture of coarse meal

In a medium sized bowl, mix the ground hazelnuts, sugar and nutmeg together

Add the egg white and mix with your hands until no dry pockets remain

With your fingers, pick up about 2 Tbsp of nut mixture and roll it into a ball

Place the ball on a baking sheet and lightly pat it down to flatten it slightly

Once all the cookies have been formed, dot each one with a whole hazelnut

Bake until the cookies are golden brown and lift cleanly from the bottom of the pan

Allow the cookies to cool 10 minutes, then dust them with icing sugar if desired

---

Toasting the nuts makes all the difference. Avoid the ground nuts found in the baking aisle at the grocery store. They've been there for ever, and their exposed surface area makes them ripe for spoilage. Nuts should be used in season and stored in the refrigerator if at all possible

Keegan's Spiced Pecans

Keegan's Spiced Pecans

Keegan's Spiced Pecans

Keegan's Spiced Pecans

KEEGAN'S SPICED PECANS

2 egg whites

½ cup Rogue Brewery Hazelnut Nectar beer (or substitute any dark, nutty beer)

1 cup sugar

1 tsp kosher salt

1 tsp ground cinnamon

½ tsp ground ginger

4 cups new-crop pecan halves

Everyone loves Keegan's nuts

Pre-heat the oven to 250F (120°C)

In a large bowl, whisk the egg whites, sugar, salt and beer together

Whisk in the spices

Toss the nuts in the beer mixture

Spread onto a large, deep baking pan

Bake, stirring every 10 minutes or so until the nuts appear dry

Remove from the pan at once and spread out the nuts on parchment to cool

Store in an airtight container at room temperature

Beware! These are highly addictive!

SWEET POTATO PECAN TART

Enough for eight 4" tarts

¾ lb sweet potatoes (not yams)

1 egg

½ cup heavy cream

½ cup brown sugar

1 tsp vanilla extract

pinch kosher salt

8 chilled, unbaked tart shells (p.135)

1 cup Keegan's spiced pecans (see p.27)

Finish this one off with a scoop of fleur-de-sel caramel ice cream. Heaven

Pre-heat the oven to 350F (165°C)

Stab the raw sweet potatoes with a fork before placing them on a baking sheet and roasting them in the oven until they are soft to the touch (30–60 minutes depending on their size)

Split the roasted sweet potatoes open and scoop out the flesh. Measure a ½ lb of roasted sweet potato into a mixing bowl and allow to cool to room temperature

Add the egg, cream, sugar, brandy and salt

Mix with a hand blender, hand-held mixer or potato masher until smooth and homogenous

Sprinkle a small handful of spiced pecans into the bottom of each tart shell

Spoon the filling on top of the nuts to nearly fill each tart shell

Bake 15 minutes, then turn and bake another 10 minutes until the filling is puffed and set

Serve warm or at room temperature, drizzled with whisky caramel (p.102) if desired

---

Sweet potatoes and yams are not the same thing. Sweet potatoes are usually small and twisty, with pale yellow flesh and tan coloured skins. Yams are typically larger, with bright orange flesh and rough brown skins. Yams, while delicious, will not give you the smooth texture you want for this recipe due to the natural latex found in their flesh. Unfortunately, yams and sweet potatoes are often mislabeled in grocery stores. It's worth it to seek out the right one!

WALNUT & ROSEMARY CARAMEL TART
Enough for eight 4" tarts

Ingredients:

- 1 cup new-crop walnut halves or pieces
- ¼ lb unsalted butter (1 stick)
- ¾ cup granulated sugar
- 3 Tbsp unpasteurized honey
- 3 Tbsp golden cane syrup
- 1 cup heavy cream
- ¼ tsp Mexican vanilla extract
- 1 large sprig fresh rosemary
- ¼ tsp kosher salt
- 8 chilled, unbaked tart shells (p.135)

The rosemary and the sweet earthiness of the walnuts balances the sweetness of the caramel

Pre-heat the oven to 350F (165°C)

Place the shelled walnuts on a baking sheet and roast them in theoven until they are aromatic and lightly browned (3–6 minutes). Set aside

Over medium heat, melt the butter in a medium saucepan

Add the sugar, honey and syrup and stir until the sugar dissolves

Turn the heat to high, and cook until the mixture is a deep amber colour. Do not stir!

Remove from the heat and whisk in the cream. Be careful, it will bubble up and release a lot of steam!

Place back on the stove at medium heat and whisk until smooth

Remove from the heat and add the vanilla, rosemary and salt

Allow the mixture to infuse for 30 minutes, then remove the rosemary

Fill each tart shell with walnuts, then spoon the caramel overtop

Bake 20 minutes, then turn and bake another 5–10 minutes until the filling has bubbled right to the center.

Remove the tart rings while the filling is still warm, then serve at room temperature

---

Seek out fresh, new-crop walnuts, it makes all the difference in the world! Most people claim not to like walnuts because they have unfortunately only ever eaten old ones that have been sitting around forever on grocery warehouse shelves

HONEY TANGERINE SORBET

Makes about 2 pints (1 litre) of sorbet

4–6 large honey tangerines

1 cup unpasteurized honey

1 cup hot water

A very talented chef told me this was the best sorbet he'd ever tasted. I thought it would be nice to share

Zest 2 of the tangerines with a rasp into a stainless steel or glass bowl

Juice the tangerines into the same bowl, right over top of the zest

Strain the juice, measuring out 2 cups (drink any extra!)

Add the honey to the juice

Add the water, stirring until the honey is dissolved

Chill uncovered in the refrigerator until completely cooled

Follow the instructions on your ice cream maker, removing the sorbet when it looks like a thick slush

Freeze at least 4 hours to allow the sorbet to set

You may have trouble scooping this one, as its texture is a little different. What matters, though, is how delicious it is!

Honey tangerines are found in cold winter months and feature a bright orange juice and a heady fragrance. Seek them out in Asian markets

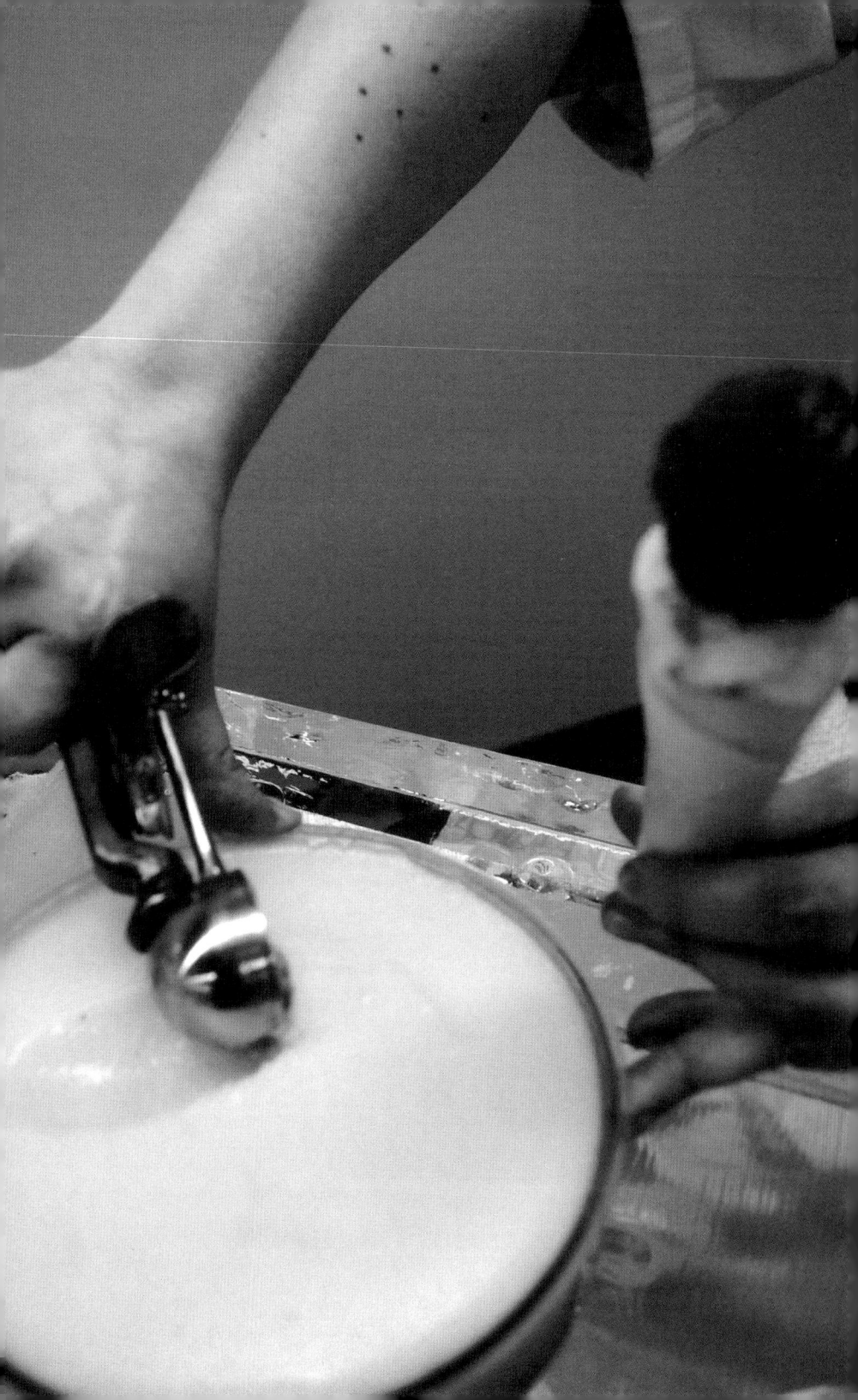

CARROT CHIFFON CAKE WITH MAPLE FROSTING
Makes a 4-layer 7" cake

Light and fluffy, this cake is a departure from dense, heavy carrot cake, but it retains the signature spices

If you'd prefer cream cheese to the maple frosting, you can layer the cake with cherry cheesecake tart filling (p.80) instead of frosting it

CARROT CHIFFON CAKE

- 1 ¼ cups cake flour, measured then sifted
- 2/3 cups granulated sugar
- 2 tsp baking powder
- ½ tsp kosher salt
- ½ tsp ground cinnamon
- 1/8 tsp ground nutmeg
- pinch ground cloves
- pinch ground allspice
- 3 egg yolks
- ½ cup fresh carrot juice
- ½ tsp vanilla extract
- 1/3 cup cold-pressed canola oil
- ½ cup shredded organic carrots
- 5 egg whites
- ¼ tsp cream of tartar (optional)
- 2 Tbsp granulated sugar

CAKE

Pre-heat the oven to 350F (165°C)

Grease two 7" straight-sided cake pans and line the bottoms with parchment rounds

In a large mixing bowl, combine all the dry ingredients with a whisk until they are evenly blended. Set aside

In a separate bowl, whisk the egg yolks, carrot juice and vanilla together

Add the oil to the yolk mixture in a steady stream, whisking constantly

Add the shredded carrot to the yolk mixture (you can also add up to ¼ cup each of raisins and nuts if you wish). Set aside

In the bowl of a mixer, whip the egg whites with the cream of tartar on medium speed until they start to look foamy

With the mixer still running, add the remaining granulated sugar in a steady stream

Continue whipping the egg whites until they form soft peaks

continued...

Juice the carrots yourself or look for fresh carrot juice in the smoothie section at the grocery store

Carrot Chiffon Cake Continued

Now, add the yolk mixture to the dry mixture and mix with a rubber spatula until no dry spots remain. Gently fold ½ of the egg whites into the batter

Even more gently, fold the remaining egg whites in, being careful not to bang the bowl on the counter

Carefully divide the batter between the two pans

Bake on the center rack of the oven for 20 minutes, then quickly and gently turn them around

Continue baking until a probe inserted in the center comes out clean (another 10–15 minutes)

Allow the cakes to rest 10 minutes before turning them out of the pan and setting them on cooling racks

Do not cut the cakes until they have completely cooled to room temperature!

Chiffon cake is a style of light and fluffy cake made with oil rather than butter. If you think about it, it's only natural that a cake made with a liquid rather than a solid would be lighter and fluffier

Carrot Chiffon Cake Continued

MAPLE FROSTING

1 cup whole milk

½ tsp kosher salt

3 Tbsp all-purpose flour

½ lb room temperature unsalted butter (2 sticks)

1 cup maple sugar (or substitute packed brown sugar)

¼ cup dark maple syrup

Sweet and subtle, this frosting tastes like autumn

FROSTING

Measure the milk and salt into a small, heavy bottomed saucepan

Whisk the flour into the milk and cook over medium heat, whisking constantly until the mixture bubbles and thickens

Remove from the heat and cover the surface with parchment or plastic wrap so that it doesn't develop a skin

Allow the milk mixture to cool to hand temperature

In the bowl of a mixer using the whisk attachment, beat the butter until creamy

Gradually add the sugar, beating until fluffy and lightened in colour

Add the maple syrup in a thin stream, scraping the sides of the bowl as necessary

Add the milk mixture and beat until smooth. If the mixture is too warm, it will look thin and soupy, if it is too cold, it will look curdled

If it is too warm, chill it in the refrigerator for 10 minutes and beat it again

If it is too cold, just keep beating it, and eventually it will become smooth, fluffy, and noticeably paler in colour

---

The best maple syrup for cooking is the lowest-grade. It has the boldest flavour and darkest colour owing to the high concentration of minerals. You can sometimes find grade "D" maple syrup in health food stores, and it is completely worth seeking out

Carrot Chiffon Cake Continued

ASSEMBLY

Using a serrated slicer, level the tops of each cake, then split each cake into two equal layers

Spread a layer of maple frosting over the bottom layer of cake, then top it with another layer of cake, repeating until you have a four-layer cake

Spread a thin layer of frosting on the outside of the cake and chill until the frosting is firm

Coat the cake in a thicker layer of frosting, smoothing out any uneven areas and leveling the top if required

If desired, pipe decorations on the top or sides of the cake, or decorate it with fresh seasonal fruit, carrot curls, or spiced nuts

FLEUR-DE-SEL CARAMEL ICE CREAM
Makes about 2 pints (1 litre) of ice cream

1/3 cup granulated sugar

2/3 cup heavy cream

2/3 cup whole milk

8 egg yolks

1/8 tsp fleur-de-sel

fleur-de-sel to taste

Salt and caramel, one of the ultimate flavour combinations

Cook the sugar in a heavy-bottomed pot over medium-high heat, scraping the bottom of the pot constantly with a wooden spoon, until it turns a dark amber colour

Pour the cream and milk over the caramelized sugar, whisking constantly, and reduce the heat to medium

In a separate bowl, whip the yolks and salt together until smooth, fluffy and lightened in colour

Whisk the hot cream mixture into the yolks a bit at a time until they are warmed

Whisk the warm yolk mixture back into the remaining hot cream in the pot

Cook over medium heat, stirring constantly until the mixture coats the back of a wooden spoon

Pass through a fine mesh strainer into a bowl set in an ice bath to stop the cooking process immediately

Chill in the refrigerator at least 8 hours

Taste the mixture and add more salt if you wish

Follow the instructions on your ice cream maker, removing the ice cream when it looks like a thick milkshake

Freeze at least 4 hours to allow the ice cream to set

Any coarse salt can be used, although fleur-de-sel is my preference because its large crystals remain present in the finished ice cream

Be very cautious making the caramel. The sugar is extremely hot and will cause the cream and milk to release hot steam on contact. Do not make when distracted!

SPRING

There's something magical about the first bundle of rhubarb in spring. When it arrives, you know that the first strawberries aren't far behind, and somehow the world looks a little sunnier.

Springtime is all about celebrating birth and rebirth, with traditions revolving around love, bunnies, nature and motherhood.

Lemon desserts are featured prominently in spring. There's nothing like a scrape of lemon zest to evoke the freshness of spring, waking up the senses just as the earth awakens from her winter slumber.

Exotic fruits are in their prime this time of year given that North American springtime takes place at the same time as the harvest time in the southern hemisphere.

Calves are born in spring, and dairy cattle are just starting to go out to pasture. Milk tastes sweeter and the creaminess of buttermilk, cheese and cream balances the bite of the tangy first fruits of the year.

PUNK ROCK RHUBARB FOOL

Enough for eight people

1 lb fresh rhubarb stems, chopped into ½ cm pieces

1 cup sugar

1 cup dry white wine

¼ of a small red beet, peeled

2 green cardamom pods, crushed

¼ vanilla bean, scraped

4 cups (1 litre) Chantilly cream (p.143)

A fool can be made with any fruit compote layered with Chantilly cream, and this one makes great use of the first fresh ingredient of spring!

Put a ½ lb of the rhubarb in a heavy bottomed pot with the sugar, wine, beet, cardamom and vanilla bean. Reserve the other half

Cook the rhubarb over medium-high heat

Insert a canning or food thermometer into the liquid to monitor the temperature as the mixture cooks

Boil the rhubarb compote until the temperature reads several degrees above 212F (100°C) even after stirring for a minute

Remove the mixture from the heat and add the reserved rhubarb to the hot rhubarb compote. Stir

Allow the mixture to cool to room temperature, stirring occasionally

Remove the beet, cardamom pieces and the vanilla bean

Spoon the mixture into glass dessert coupes, and layer with the Chantilly cream

Serve immediately

Rhubarb can be found all through the growing season, but it's often the first kind of fresh produce to make its way to the kitchen after the snowy months, making it a favourite spring ingredient!

The beet is only there to make it look pretty, leave it out if you don't have one handy

PASSIONFRUIT AND MANGO TART

Enough for eight 4" tarts

3 eggs

6 yolks

1 cup sugar

1 cup fresh passionfruit pulp (4–6 fruits' worth)

¾ cup cold, cubed butter (1½ sticks)

8 par-baked tart shells (p.135)

4 medium Atalfo mangos

purple basil shoots (optional)

It takes a long time to master the presentation of this beautiful tart. If you're finding it frustrating, just chop the mango and pile it on top!

Whisk the eggs and sugar together in a medium mixing bowl

Add the passionfruit pulp (include the seeds) and place over a pot of simmering water, stirring occasionally until the mixture thickens to the texture of pudding (15–30 minutes)

Remove the mixture from the heat and add the butter, whisking constantly until it is incorporated into the curd

Pass the curd through a fine mesh strainer

Pre-heat the oven to 350F (165°C)

Spoon the passionfruit curd to fill the shells half full.

Flash the tarts in the oven 5 minutes

Put the tarts in the refrigerator to cool

Peel the mangos and slice the lobes off each side of the pit

Thinly slice the mango lobes and arrange the slices to form a circular, swirly pattern and garnish with purple basil shoots if desired

Enjoy as fresh as possible

You can find Atalfo mangos, also known as long mangos, in markets from March to June. They have smooth, bright yellow skins and sweet, slippery flesh containing less fiber than most mangos. Look for ones with no black spots whose skins have a little give, but skip the wrinkled ones, they're too ripe

FROMAGE BLANC CHEESECAKE

Makes eight individual cheesecakes

2 lbs fromage blanc
¾ cups granulated sugar
4 eggs

This recipe was inspired by the best dessert I've ever had, which consisted of nothing more than a bowl full of fresh cheese, a dollop of heavy cream, and a sugar shaker

Preheat the oven to 200F (95°C)

In a mixer, using the paddle attachment, beat the cream cheese and sugar together until smooth

Add the eggs one at a time, scraping the sides of the bowl in between each addition

Spoon the mixture in to individual sized silicone molds

Bake for 1 hour

Allow the cheesecakes to chill completely in the refrigerator before turning out of the molds

Serve with fresh fruit and lemon lavender shortbread (p.50)

To go crazy, add a scoop of buttermilk ice cream (p.53)

Fromage blanc means "white cheese" in English, and is the phrase used in French for unripened cheese. In North America, we've replaced it with cream cheese, which if you read the ingredients on the side of the package, contains a lot more than just cheese. If you have a really good cheesemonger in your city, you may be able to find fromage blanc, but I make my own using cultures I purchase from the New England Cheesemaking Company. They're my favourite hippies, check out their website!

LEMON LAVENDER SHORTBREAD

Makes about 40 - 2 ½ inch cookies

Ingredients:

- ½ lb cold unsalted butter, cut into cubes
- 2 ¾ cups all-purpose flour
- 1 tsp dried lavender
- 3 egg yolks
- ¾ cup granulated sugar
- 3 Tbsp icing sugar
- 1/8 tsp kosher salt
- ½ tsp vanilla extract
- 1 tsp fresh lemon juice
- 1 tsp fresh lemon zest

When baked, these cookies should have a sandy, crumbly texture and a fragrant, lively flavour

Preheat the oven to 350F (165°C)

In the bowl of a mixer using the paddle attachment, blend the butter, flour and lavender together on low speed until the butter until the mixture is the texture of sand

In a separate small bowl, mix the yolks, sugar, salt, vanilla and lemon juice and zest together to make a thick paste

Add the yolk paste to the flour mixture and mix on low speed until the mixture comes together as a heavy dough

Wrap the dough in plastic wrap and refrigerate until fully chilled and firm

Roll out the dough, using as little flour as possible. You may wish to roll it between two pieces of parchment instead of on the counter

Cut the cookies using your favourite cutter, or just cut them into squares or triangles with a knife

Place the cut cookies on a baking sheet and chill them in the fridge or freezer for 10 minutes before baking them

Bake the cookies until they are just starting to brown along the edges, 8–10 minutes

Remove the cookies to a rack and allow them to cool 10 minutes before serving them

Culinary lavender is available in many specialty stores, or if you're feeling really ambitious, you can grow some on your kitchen windowsill!

NECT

BUTTERMILK ICE

BUTTERMILK ICE CREAM

Makes about 2 pints (1 litre) of ice cream

2/3 cup heavy cream

8 egg yolks

1/3 cup granulated sugar

2/3 cup full-fat organic buttermilk

Inspired by the best ice cream I've ever tasted (from St. John in London), the buttermilk lends a refreshing bite to this ice cream, making it a perfect match for tangy desserts or as a pairing for fresh fruit

Over medium heat in a heavy bottomed pot, warm the cream

In a separate bowl, whip the yolks and sugar together until smooth, fluffy and lightened in colour

Whisk the hot cream into the yolks a bit at a time until they are warmed

Whisk the warm yolk mixture back into the remaining hot cream in the pot

Cook over medium heat, stirring constantly until the mixture coats the back of a wooden spoon

Pass through a fine mesh strainer into a bowl set in an ice bath to stop the cooking process immediately

Add the buttermilk to the strained custard

Chill in the refrigerator at least 8 hours

Follow the instructions on your ice cream maker, removing the ice cream when it looks like a thick milkshake

Freeze at least 4 hours to allow the ice cream to set

This recipe is so simple that the ingredients really need to be top-rate to make it sing. I make my own buttermilk (thank you New England Cheesemaking Company!), but good local organic buttermilk will work if you don't feel that ambitious. Don't skimp on the milk and eggs either, make sure they're the freshest, highest quality that you can find!

FRAGRANT LEMON TART

Enough for eight 4" tarts

6–8 fresh lemons

3 eggs

6 yolks

1 cup sugar

¾ cup cold, cubed butter (1½ sticks)

¼ tsp orange flower water

8 par-baked tart shells (p.135)

candied lemon zest (p.145)

Perfect with a sweet berry sorbet

Zest the lemons into a small bowl using a rasp or microplane

Squeeze the lemon juice out of the lemons right on top of the zest, then measure the juice (make lemonade with the rest or save it for later!)

Whisk the eggs and sugar together in a medium mixing bowl

Add 1 cup of the unstrained lemon juice and place over a pot of simmering water, stirring occasionally until the mixture thickens to the texture of pudding (15–30 minutes)

Remove the mixture from the heat and add the butter, whisking constantly until it is incorporated into the curd

Pass the curd through a fine mesh strainer

Pre-heat the oven to 350F (165°C)

Spoon the lemon curd into the shells until they are full

Flash the tarts in the oven 5 minutes

Put the tarts in the refrigerator to cool

If desired, before the tarts are completely chilled, add a knot of candied lemon for garnish

---

Juicing the lemons right into the zest captures the lemon oil that is released from the lemon skin when it is zested. It also allows the flavour from the zest to infuse into the juice, and keeps the zest from drying out. Try it, it's my not-so-secret secret

RUM & RAISIN ROUNDIES

Makes about 3 dozen cookies

260 g raisins or currants

dark rum

½ lb softened unsalted butter (2 sticks)

1 ½ cups granulated sugar

2 tsp kosher salt

4 eggs

½ cup whole milk

4 tsp vanilla extract

3 tsp lemon liqueur (like limoncello)

4 ¾ cups all-purpose flour

1 ¾ cups cornstarch

4 tsp baking powder

½ tsp salt

icing sugar

There's something Easter-y about these cookies, they're the perfect thing to eat with tea and tiny sandwiches

In a small covered bowl, soak the raisins in rum overnight at room temperature

Drain the raisins, reserving the rum

Pre-heat the oven to 350F (165°C)

Cream the butter, sugar and salt in a mixer using the paddle attachment until fluffy and light in colour

Add the eggs, one at a time, followed by the milk, vanilla, limoncello and 4 tsp of the soaking rum, scraping down the bowl as needed

Sift in the flour, cornstarch, baking powder and salt, then mix until smooth

Fold in the drained currants

With your fingers, pick up about 2 Tbsp of dough and roll it into a ball

Place the ball on a baking sheet and lightly pat it down to flatten it slightly

Bake until the cookies are golden brown and lift cleanly from the bottom of the pan

Allow the cookies to cool 10 minutes, then dust them with icing sugar if desired

If you have some extra candied lemon zest (p.145), chop a bit up and throw it in the batter

LEMON BERRY CHIFFON CAKE

Makes a 4-layer 7" cake

LEMON CHIFFON CAKE

1 ¼ cups cake flour, measured then sifted

2/3 cups granulated sugar

2 tsp baking powder

½ tsp kosher salt

3 egg yolks

½ cup fresh squeezed lemon juice

¾ tsp fresh lemon zest

½ tsp vanilla extract

1/3 cup cold-pressed canola oil

5 egg whites

¼ tsp cream of tartar (optional)

2 Tbsp granulated sugar

Light and bursting with lemon flavour, this cake was once named the best thing to eat in the city

Use whatever berries are most in season, but I find raspberries deliver the most sublime result

<u>CAKE</u>

Pre-heat the oven to 350F (165°C)

Grease two 7" straight-sided cake pans and line the bottoms with parchment rounds

In a large mixing bowl, combine all the dry ingredients with a whisk until they are evenly blended. Set aside

In a separate bowl, whisk the egg yolks, lemon juice, zest and vanilla together

Add the oil to the yolk mixture in a steady stream, whisking constantly

In the bowl of a mixer, whip the egg whites with the cream of tartar on medium speed until they start to look foamy

With the mixer still running, add the remaining granulated sugar in a steady stream

Continue whipping the egg whites until they form soft peaks

Now, add the yolk mixture to the dry mixture and mix with a rubber spatula until no dry spots remain

Gently fold ½ of the egg whites into the batter

continued...

Cold-pressed canola oil can sometimes add a grassy flavour to your cake. If you prefer a pure lemon flavour, you can substitute a more neutral oil

Lemon Berry Chiffon Cake Continued

Even more gently, fold the remaining egg whites in, being careful not to bang the bowl on the counter

Carefully divide the batter between the two pans

Bake on the center rack of the oven for 20 minutes, then quickly and gently turn them around

Continue baking until a probe inserted in the center comes out clean (another 10–15 minutes)

Allow the cakes to rest 10 minutes before turning them out of the pan and setting them on cooling racks

Do not cut the cakes until they have completely cooled to room temperature!

Lemon Berry Chiffon Cake Continued

LEMON FROSTING

1 cup whole milk

½ tsp kosher salt

3 Tbsp all-purpose flour

½ lb room temperature unsalted butter (2 sticks)

1 cup granulated sugar

6 Tbsp fragrant lemon curd (p.54)

This frosting can be quite soft, so be careful to keep it cool on those hot summer days!

FROSTING

Measure the milk and salt into a small, heavy bottomed saucepan

Whisk the flour into the milk and cook over medium heat, whisking constantly until the mixture bubbles and thickens

Remove from the heat and cover the surface with parchment or plastic wrap so that it doesn't develop a skin

Allow the milk mixture to cool to hand temperature

In the bowl of a mixer using the whisk attachment, beat the butter until creamy

Gradually add the sugar, beating until fluffy and lightened in colour

Add the lemon curd, scraping the sides of the bowl as necessary

Add the milk mixture and beat until smooth. If the mixture is too warm, it will look thin and soupy, if it is too cold, it will look curdled

If it is too warm, chill it in the refrigerator for 10 minutes and beat it again

If it is too cold, just keep beating it, and eventually it will become smooth, fluffy, and noticeably paler in colour

It may seem like a lot of effort to make a batch of lemon curd just to use in this recipe, however, lemon curd keeps quite well in the refrigerator and can be saved for making mousse, tarts or just for spreading on toast!

Lemon Berry Chiffon Cake Continued

LEMON MOUSSE

2 cups white chocolate mousse (p.138)

¼ cup fragrant lemon curd (p.54)

You can flavour the mousse with the curd left over from making the frosting or a batch of tarts

MOUSSE

Gently fold the cold lemon curd into the chilled mousse

If you prefer more berry than lemon in your cake, you can substitute ¼ cup of berry conserve (p.75) for the lemon curd in the recipe

Lemon Berry Chiffon Cake Continued

1 ½–2 cups fresh berries (try raspberries, blackberries, strawberries or blueberries)

ASSEMBLY

Using a serrated slicer, level the tops of each cake, then split each cake into two equal layers

Fill a large-tipped piping bag with frosting and pipe a thick ring of frosting around the edge of the bottom layer of cake

Carefully place a ring of fresh berries around the inner edge of the frosting ring, embedding them side-by-side in the frosting to form a "necklace"

Spoon lemon mousse into the center, spreading it out with the back of the spoon to fill in the center

Top with another layer of cake and repeat until you have a four-layer cake (for a more stable cake, skip the berries in the center layer)

Spread a thin layer of frosting on the outside of the cake and chill until the frosting is firm

Coat the cake in a thicker layer of frosting, smoothing out any uneven areas and leveling the top if required

If desired, pipe decorations on the top or sides of the cake, or decorate it with fresh berries and candied lemon zest (p.154)

This way of assembling a cake is tricky. If you find it too difficult, skip the frosting and just spread mousse between the layers and dot it with berries throughout. It'll be more rustic and just as delicious

SUMMER

The bounty of fresh fruit available in summer makes it hard to even think about cooking. Why adulterate the natural perfection of a fresh raspberry or a ripe fig?

In summer, recipes lean toward simplicity, displaying the natural beauty and flavours of fresh fruits rather than manipulating them.

Frozen desserts are a natural choice, ice cream and sorbet cool the tongue and make you feel like a kid, but you can enjoy grown-up flavours such as blue cheese if you want to!

Stone fruits like peaches, apricots and cherries attract wasps and dribble their juice down our chins, asking for nothing more than a lick of honey or a dollop of cream to achieve absolute perfection.

It's worth it to put the warmth of the summer sun in jars and save some for the rest of the year. It's in summer that we start preserving, freezing and canning berries, jams and conserves.

HONEY ICE CREAM

Makes about 2 pints (1 litre) of ice cream

2/3 cup heavy cream

2/3 cup whole milk

8 egg yolks

1/3 cup unpasteurized honey

The honey, in addition to flavouring the ice cream, lends it a beautiful smooth texture

Over medium heat in a heavy bottomed pot, warm the cream and milk together

In a separate bowl, whip the yolks and honey together until smooth, fluffy and lightened in colour

Whisk the hot cream mixture into the yolks a bit at a time until they are warmed

Whisk the warm yolk mixture back into the remaining hot cream in the pot

Cook over medium heat, stirring constantly until the mixture coats the back of a wooden spoon

Pass through a fine mesh strainer into a bowl set in an ice bath to stop the cooking process immediately

Chill in the refrigerator at least 8 hours

Follow the instructions on your ice cream maker, removing the ice cream when it looks like a thick milkshake

Freeze at least 4 hours to allow the ice cream to set

The flavour of the honey comes from the flowers the bees are feeding on. I've made this recipe with alfalfa, clover, fireweed, tupelo and even buckwheat honey, each batch turning out with its own character and charm

BLACKBERRY & PASSIONFRUIT MOUSSE TART
Enough for eight 4" tarts

2 cups white chocolate mousse (p.138)

¼ cup passionfruit curd (p.46)

4 cups fresh blackberries

vanilla bean syrup (p.140)

8 fully-baked tart shells (p.135)

The double-whammy sweet&sour combo of the blackberries and passionfruit combines with the richness of the cream to turn out just dreamy

Gently fold the white chocolate mousse and curd together

Spoon the passionfruit mousse into the base of each tart shell

Taste the blackberries and toss them with vanilla syrup if desired

Carefully arrange a ring of blackberries around the outside of the tart shell to form a "necklace" of blackberries

Randomly tumble the remaining blackberries into the center of the tarts to fill them in

Enjoy within 2 days

When ripe, blackberries are a marvelous treat. Look for fat, juicy ones mid to late summer and avoid firm ones with small, tight drupelets (the little orbs)

PEACH COBBLER

Makes 1 9x12 inch pan

PEACH FILLING

3 ½ lbs ripe peaches

3 Tbsp cornstarch

Unpasteurized honey, to taste

COBBLER BISCUITS

3 1/3 cups all purpose flour

7 Tbsp granulated sugar

3 Tbsp baking powder

¼ tsp kosher salt

¾ cups cold unsalted butter, cubed (1½ sticks)

1 1/3 cups heavy cream

heavy cream for brushing

raw sugar for sprinkling

Cobbler is a fruit dessert with a biscuit topping. What I love about it is the underside of the biscuit layer. It tastes like a pre-jammed scone

You can substitute any fruit for this recipe

Leave the peaches unpeeled or skin them if you prefer, then cut them into even slices, removing the flesh from the pits

Taste the fruit to see if it is sweet enough, if you would prefer it sweeter, add honey until it tastes the way you'd like

Toss the sliced fruit with the cornstarch until no white powder remains and place in an even layer in the bottom of a greased pan

Preheat the oven to 350F (165°C)

In the bowl of a mixer, combine the dry ingredients together with the paddle attachment

Add the cold butter, and blend on low speed until the mixture is the consistency of coarse meal

Add the heavy cream and mix until the dough comes together and pulls away from the sides of the bowl

Working quickly, divide the dough into 16 pieces and pat each one into a rough disc shape by sandwiching it between your hands. The biscuits should be rustic in appearance

continued...

Any fruit can be substituted for the peaches in this recipe. A good rule of thumb for the filling is that for every pound of prepared fruit (peeled, stoned or skinned), you will need approximately 1 Tbsp of cornstarch

Peach Cobbler Continued

Lay the biscuits on top of the peach filling at regular intervals. The biscuit should cover the filling, but don't be concerned about gaps between the biscuits, they will spread

Place the pan in the fridge for 15 minutes to chill. It can be left there up to 8 hours

Brush the tops of the biscuits with heavy cream, then sprinkle with raw sugar

Bake for 20 minutes, then turn the pan in the oven

Continue baking until the biscuits are golden brown and the filling is bubbling (another 15–20 minutes)

Allow to cool at room temperature

It's so tempting to eat cobbler the moment it comes out of the oven, and indeed, it is delicious, but it's at its very best the next day once the biscuit has absorbed the delicious fruity goodness

BERRY CONSERVE

Equal parts (by weight) trimmed berries and granulated sugar

This simple recipe will allow you to take advantage of the summer's bounty through the whole year!

Combine the fruit and sugar together in a heavy-bottomed pot

Let the mixture sit at room temperature, stirring occasionally to allow the sugar to begin extracting moisture from the fruit (yay osmosis!)

Once all the sugar is moistened, place the pot on the stove and bring the liquid to a boil

Insert a canning or food thermometer into the liquid to monitor the temperature as the mixture cooks

Boil the fruit and sugar together until the temperature reads several degrees above 212F (100°C) even after stirring for a minute

Allow the mixture to cool before transferring to clean storage containers

If canning, follow the canning equipment instructions

If not canning, store the conserve in the refrigerator up to six months

Use strawberries, blackberries, raspberries, gooseberries, blueberries, or just about any flavourful fruit with this recipe

The sugar acts as a natural preservative, but just like any jam, if it's in an unsealed container it should be stored in the fridge

KEY LIME & BLUEBERRY TART

Enough for eight 4" tarts

The intensity of the lime curd stands in contrast to the summery sweetness of the fresh and preserved blueberries

3 eggs

6 yolks

1 cup sugar

¾ cups fresh-squeezed key lime juice

¾ cup cold, cubed butter (1½ sticks)

½ cup blueberry conserve (p.75)

fresh blueberries

vanilla bean syrup (p.140)

8 par-baked tart shells (p.135)

Whisk the eggs and sugar together in a medium mixing bowl

Add the lime juice and place over a pot of simmering water, stirring occasionally until the mixture thickens to the texture of pudding (15–30 minutes)

Remove the mixture from the heat and add the butter, whisking constantly until it is incorporated into the curd

Pass the curd through a fine mesh strainer

Pre-heat the oven to 350F (165°C)

Spread a layer of blueberry conserve on the bottom of each tart shell

Spoon the lime curd on top of the conserve until the shells are ¾ full

Flash the tarts in the oven 5 minutes

Put the tarts in the refrigerator to cool

Wash the blueberries, then toss them with vanilla syrup to glaze

Arrange the blueberries on top of the chilled lime curd

Enjoy within 2 days

If the idea of juicing the key limes is giving you nightmares, feel free to use regular limes. The flavour won't be as biting, but you won't have to spend an afternoon juicing tiny limes

SUMMER BERRY SORBET

Makes about 2 pints (1 litre) of sorbet

1 lb hulled strawberries, blueberries, raspberries, blackberries, or any combination thereof

1 cup boiling water

1 cup granulated sugar

This recipe is a great use for soft, sweet overripe berries

Wash the fruit carefully and place it in a large measuring or blender cup

In a separate bowl, pour the boiling water over the sugar and stir to until the sugar dissolves

Pour the warm syrup over the berries

Puree using a hand or stationary blender until no lumps remain

Pass the mixture through a fine mesh strainer and chill uncovered in the refrigerator until completely cooled

Follow the instructions on your ice cream maker, removing the sorbet when it looks like a thick slush

Freeze at least 4 hours to allow the sorbet to set

Scoop!

When I was a baby chef, I always wanted to make crazy foods, experimenting with every flavour in the book. Star anise! Tarragon! Pine nuts! Soursop! Like a mad scientist, I searched for the most unusual combinations I could find. Eventually though, like so many chefs before me, I came back to true, clean flavours. As interesting as a grapefruit and rosemary sheep's milk sherbet might be, there's nothing as pure and delicious as a simple fresh raspberry sorbet

CHERRY CHEESECAKE TART

Enough for eight 4" tarts

1 cup white chocolate mousse (p.138)

1 cup homemade mascarpone (p.139)—you can substitute fromage blanc or good quality storebought mascarpone

1 lb sweet cherries, halved and pitted

vanilla bean syrup (p.140)

8 fully-baked tart shells (p.135)

The filling, while not true cheesecake, evokes the flavour with its rich, creamy cheesiness

Gently fold the white chocolate mousse and mascarpone together

Taste the cherries and glaze them with the syrup to taste

Spoon the mascarpone mousse into the base of each tart shell

Carefully arrange the cherries in a ring around the outside of the tart to form a "necklace"

Heap a small handful of cherries randomly in the center of the tart to fill it in

Enjoy immediately

Use any sweet summer cherries for this tart. Rainiers and other white cherries are delicious and look pretty, but they will brown quickly

TRIPLE RASPBERRY TART

Enough for eight 4" tarts

6 Tbsp raspberry conserve (p.75)

2 cups white chocolate mousse (p.138)

4 cups fresh raspberries

8 fully-baked tart shells (p.135)

Raspberry Conserve, Raspberry Mousse, Fresh Raspberries

Spread a heaping teaspoon of raspberry conserve in the bottom of each tart shell. Chill

Gently fold the white chocolate mousse and remaining conserve together

Spoon the raspberry mousse on top of the conserve in each tart shell

Carefully arrange a ring of raspberries around the outside of the tart shell to form a "necklace" of raspberries

Randomly tumble the remaining raspberries into the center of the tarts to fill them in

Enjoy within 2 days

Look for dark-coloured, shiny-surfaced raspberries. If they're overripe and mushy, you can throw them in the freezer and save them for sorbet or conserve

FIG & HONEY MOUSSE TART

Enough for eight 4" tarts

2 cups white chocolate mousse (p.138)

¼ cup unpasteurized honey

16 ripe fresh figs

8 fully-baked tart shells (p.135)

This tart is a showstopper. Use a mild flavoured honey, you don't want to overwhelm the delicate flavour of the figs!

Gently fold the white chocolate mousse and honey together

Spoon the honey mousse into the base of each tart shell

Trim the stems from the figs, then slice them lengthwise into 8 pieces

Carefully arrange the figs around the outside of the tart shell, pressing the cut face into the inside wall of the shell

Arrange the remaining figs in the center of the tart

Enjoy immediately

Figs are available in late summer. Seek out ones that feel heavy for their size, and are soft and squashy. They should look wet and glistening inside, and at their peak, taste like strawberry jam. Skins are eaten or discarded depending on your preference

BLUE CHEESE ICE CREAM

Makes about 2 pints (1 litre) of ice cream

2/3 cup heavy cream

2/3 cup whole milk

8 egg yolks

1/3 cup granulated sugar

150 g St. Agur cheese

This unusual ice cream really does taste like blue cheese, but balanced with sweetness and enhanced by the temperature. A really wonderful accompaniment for ripe summer fruits

Over medium heat in a heavy bottomed pot, warm the cream and milk together

In a separate bowl, whip the yolks and sugar together until smooth, fluffy and lightened in colour

Whisk the hot cream mixture into the yolks a bit at a time until they are warmed

Whisk the warm yolk mixture back into the remaining hot cream in the pot

Cook over medium heat, stirring constantly until the mixture coats the back of a wooden spoon

Pass through a fine mesh strainer into a bowl set in an ice bath to stop the cooking process immediately

Rinse the cheese under cold water and crumble it into the still-warm custard

Stir until most of the cheese has dissolved

Chill in the refrigerator at least 8 hours

Follow the instructions on your ice cream maker, removing the ice cream when it looks like a thick milkshake

Freeze at least 4 hours to allow the ice cream to set

St. Agur is my favourite cheese to use for this recipe. It has a smooth texture, true "blue" flavour, and isn't too salty. Other blues are delicious for eating, but not as well suited for making ice cream

HARVEST

As days grow shorter and cooler at the tail end of summer, markets start overflowing with the bounty of the season – something much more impactful than the turning of the leaves.

Apples abound, in dozens of varieties. Plums come in every size, colour and flavour. The last cherries of the season arrive: the puckery-sour ones.

So many of the foods we see every day of the year on grocery store shelves—apples, pears, grapes (or raisins), plums, even corn—are seasonal foods. As much as we can force them to grow year-round, it's when they are allowed to grow naturally and harvested in the fall that they are at their sweet, succulent best.

It's not just the fresh fruit that's at its best in autumn, it's also the nuts and dried fruits. Nuts aren't meant to sit around indefinitely. Just like fruit, they are at their tastiest right after they are plucked from their trees. Dried fruit, by the same token, is at its most delectable when it's fresh, plump and flavourful—a bite of concentrated summer sun.

APPLE PUDDING CAKE

Makes 1 9x12 inch pan

3 cups all-purpose flour

2 cups granulated sugar

1 Tbsp baking powder

¾ tsp kosher salt

1 tsp ground cinnamon

¼ tsp freshly ground nutmeg

pinch allspice

1 1/3 cups whole milk

1/3 cup canola oil

1 Tbsp vanilla extract

2 cups peeled and diced sweet apples (lady, gala, etc)

2 cups peeled and diced tart apples (granny smith, cox pippin, etc)

1 ½ cups dark brown sugar

3 cups hot apple cider or natural apple juice

This dessert is inspired by a childhood favourite: Dr. Oetker self-saucing cakes

Feel free to substitute pears, plums or other fruit for this recipe

Preheat the oven to 350F (165°C)

Combine the dry ingredients together. Set aside

Combine the wet ingredients. Set aside

Mix the wet and dry ingredients together with a rubber spatula until no dry pockets remain

Combine the apples together and add them to the batter

Spread the batter evenly over the bottom of the greased pan

Sprinkle the brown sugar over the surface of the batter

Heat the apple cider until boiling, and pour over the surface of the batter

Bake 20 minutes, then quickly and gently turn the pan in the oven

Continue baking until bubbling and set (10–20 minutes)

Serve warm with vanilla bean custard (p.142) or ice cream

Each variety of apple brings something different to the table in the flavour, tartness and texture department. I try to use as many varieties as possible, mixing tart with sweet, mealy with crisp. Don't limit yourself to just two kinds, grab as many varieties as you please!

SWEET CORN ICE CREAM

Makes about 2 pints (1 litre) of ice cream

1 cob fresh sweet corn

1-inch piece of vanilla bean, split open

2/3 cup heavy cream

2/3 cup whole milk

8 egg yolks

1/3 cup granulated sugar

Harvest corn is so sweet and creamy, it just makes sense as ice cream. My favourite with pumpkin pie!

Peel the corn and cut away the kernels. Using the back a knife, scrape the pulp from the cob

Add the vanilla, corn kernels, pulp and the cob to the milk and cream in a heavy bottomed pot and warm over medium heat

In a separate bowl, whip the yolks and honey together until smooth, fluffy and lightened in colour

Whisk the hot cream mixture into the yolks a bit at a time until they are warmed

Whisk the warm yolk mixture back into the remaining hot cream in the pot

Cook over medium heat, stirring constantly until the mixture coats the back of a wooden spoon

Pass through a fine mesh strainer into a bowl set in an ice bath to stop the cooking process immediately.

Chill in the refrigerator at least 8 hours

Follow the instructions on your ice cream maker, removing the ice cream when it looks like a thick milkshake

Freeze at least 4 hours to allow the ice cream to set

The key to this recipe is to get all the 'milk' out of the cob. When you strain the ice cream, make sure that you scrape the cob a second time to get all the delicious goodness out of it

SOUR CHERRY CRUMBLE TART

Enough for eight 4" tarts

1 lb sour cherries, pitted
2 cups granulated sugar
1 Tbsp cornstarch
¼ cup unsalted butter (½ a stick)
1/3 cup brown sugar
½ cup rolled oats
½ cup all-purpose flour
pinch salt
pinch ground cinnamon
8 par-baked tart shells (p.135)

This puckery-delicious late summer treat is well worth digging out the cherry pitter!

Toss the sour cherries with the sugar and cornstarch in a medium pot

Let them sit, stirring occasionally until enough liquid has been extracted from the cherries to moisten the sugar and dissolve the cornstarch

Cook over medium-high heat, stirring occasionally until the mixture boils. Remove from the heat and set aside

In the meantime, heat the oven to 350F (165°C)

Melt the butter, and combine it with the brown sugar, oats, flour, salt and cinnamon

Spoon the cooled cherry mixture into the tart shells until ¾ full, then top with the crumble mixture

Bake in the oven until the cherry mixture bubbles again, 10–15 minutes

Serve warm

Sour cherries are the ones traditionally used for pies and preserves. They tend to be bright red in colour and have a distinct puckery bite to them. They can be hard to find in my native Alberta, but a small crop appears every fall and I always pounce on them. If you can't find fresh, seek out frozen ones, they work quite well

OATMEAL RAISIN COOKIES

Makes about 3 dozen cookies

1 cup + 2 Tbsp all-purpose flour	**When these cookies are baking, I can't resist pressing my nose against the glass in sheer anticipation**
1 cup + 2 Tbsp rolled oats	Pre-heat the oven to 350F (165°C)
1 cup brown sugar	In the bowl of a mixer, blend the flour, oats, brown sugar, soda, powder and salt together with the paddle attachment
¾ tsp baking soda	
¾ tsp baking powder	
½ tsp kosher salt	Blend in the butter until thoroughly combined
2 Tbsp softened unsalted butter (¼ stick)	Add the liquid and raisins and combine on low speed until evenly distributed
1 egg	Scoop the dough into heaping teaspoons, and place on a baking sheet at least 2 cm. apart
4 tsp water	
1 tsp vanilla	Bake until the center of the cookies have puffed and the tops are golden brown (10–12 minutes)
1 cup raisins (or substitute whatever you prefer: chocolate chips, dried fruit, toffee chips, candies, etc)	Enjoy warm with a glass of milk

Make sure you're using real rolled oats rather than oatmeal for making this recipe. Avoid any product that advertises itself as "instant"

DAMSON PLUM COMPOTE

Makes about 2 cups of compote

½ lb pitted damson plums

2 cups granulated sugar

1 cinnamon stick, broken

1 orange, peel-on, sliced into quarters

Pair it with pumpkin cheesecake and sweet corn ice cream, or just eat it by the spoonful!

Combine the plums, sugar, cinnamon and orange pieces together in a heavy-bottomed pot

Let the mixture sit at room temperature, stirring occasionally to allow the sugar to begin extracting moisture from the plums

Once all the sugar is moistened, place the pot on the stove and bring the liquid to a boil

Insert a canning or food thermometer into the liquid to monitor the temperature as the mixture cooks

Boil until the temperature reads above 212 F (100°C) even after stirring for a minute

Allow the mixture to cool before removing the cinnamon and orange pieces and transferring to clean storage containers

If canning, follow the canning equipment instructions

If not canning, store the conserve in the refrigerator up to six months

Damson plums are tiny, ugly and sour. If you try them on their own, they taste awful, but they are uniquely qualified to be cooked into the most beautiful, delicious and versatile compote around. Don't pass them by during their short autumn season!

ROASTED APPLE & CHESTNUT TART

Enough for eight 4" tarts

¼ lb French or Italian chestnuts, shelled

½ cup all-purpose flour

¼ lb room temperature unsalted butter (1 stick)

½ cup granulated sugar

2 eggs

8 chilled, unbaked tart shells (p.135)

4–6 Jonagold or other sweet autumn apples

This earthy, rustic tart tastes amazing, but comes into its own served warm with a scoop of homemade ice cream

Pre-heat the oven to 350F (165°C)

Place the shelled chestnuts on a baking sheet and roast them in the oven until they are dry, aromatic and lightly browned (10–15 minutes)

Allow the chestnuts to cool slightly then crumble them into the flour and toss to coat

Place the butter and the sugar together in a mixing bowl and beat with the paddle attachment until fluffy and light in colour

Add the eggs one at a time, scraping down the sides of the bowl with each addition

Add the flour and nuts and mix until there are no lumps of flour remaining and the mixture resembles chunky peanut butter

Spoon into the tart shells until 1/3 full and layer with thinly sliced apple.

Bake 15 minutes, then turn and bake another 10 minutes until the apples are browned and the filling has puffed up.

Serve warm

Don't be lured in by inexpensive Asian chestnuts! They are bitter and not suitable for sweet preparations. Shell out for the European ones

If you are lucky enough to get chestnuts with their shells still on, lay them on a baking sheet and put them in a hot (400F+) oven until the shells crack open. Then, with a sturdy knife or nutcracker, finish the job and peel the shells away while the nuts are still warm

Double

STICKY TOFFEE PUDDING WITH WHISKY CARAMEL SAUCE

Makes 1 9x12 inch pan

STICKY TOFFEE PUDDING

½ lb Medjool dates, pits in

2 cups water

2 tsp vanilla extract

2 tsp baking soda

6 cups all-purpose flour

2 tsp baking powder

½ tsp kosher salt

½ cup + 2 Tbsp softened unsalted butter (1 ¼ sticks)

1 ½ cups granulated sugar

2 eggs

The secret is peeling the dates

Bring a large pot of water to a rolling boil

Prepare a large bowl full of ice water

Add the dates to the boiling water and let them boil for approximately one minute until all of the skins are split

Scoop the dates out of the water with a strainer and drop them into the ice water

Remove the skins and pits from the dates and set the date meat aside (you should have about 1/3 lb or 150g)

In a medium sized heavy-bottomed pot, combine the date meat, vanilla, baking soda and water, and bring to a boil. Simmer 2 minutes (the mixture will bubble up quite a bit and look gross, strange and greenish)

Allow the date mixture to cool to room temperature

Preheat the oven to 350F (165°C)

— Combine the flour, baking powder and salt together

— Cream the butter and sugar in a mixer using the paddle attachment until fluffy and light in colour

— Add the eggs one at a time, scraping down the sides of the bowl with each addition

1 — Add one third of the flour mixture and mix until combined

2 — Add half the date mixture and mix until combined, scraping the bowl as needed

continued...

There are a million recipes for sticky toffee pudding, but what they all have in common is dates. Dates give the dessert its sweetness and signature texture. Oh, and in the UK, "pudding" means "dessert", which is its definition in this recipe

Sticky Toffee Pudding Continued

 Repeat the previous two steps: dry ingredients, then dates, finishing with dry ingredients

Spread the batter evenly into a greased or parchment lined pan

Bake for 20 minutes, then turn the pan in the oven

Bake another 15–25 minutes until a probe inserted in the center comes out clean

While the cake is baking, prepare one recipe's worth of whisky caramel sauce (p.102)

As soon as the cake is out of the oven, cut it into the desired portions with a sharp knife. Do not remove them from the pan

Ladle the warm sauce over the warm cake and allow it to absorb. Brush the cake with the sauce to ensure maximum absorption

Sticky Toffee Pudding Continued

WHISKY CARAMEL SAUCE

2 ¾ cups granulated sugar

½ lb cold cubed unsalted butter (2 sticks)

1 ½ cups whipping cream

¼ cup good quality whisky

This sauce is great on just about ANYTHING

Measure out all the ingredients in advance and have them ready by the stove

Cook the sugar in a clean, dry, heavy-bottomed pot over medium-high heat

As the sugar melts, move it around the bottom of the pot with a wooden spoon, mixing the dry sugar with the molten sugar

Once all the sugar is molten, continue stirring gently until it has turned a deep, reddish brown

Immediately turn off the heat and whisk in the cold butter (be careful, it will splatter and release steam. Keep your hands out of the way!)

Once all the butter is melted (it may be a bit oily), whisk in the cream (be careful, the mixture will still be VERY hot)

If the mixture has crystallized, allow the heat of the caramel to dissolve the crystals by stirring them into the hot liquid. If necessary, turn the heat back on to low and allow the mixture to warm enough to dissolve the crystals

Stir in the whisky and pour over any food to make it taste soooo good!

As you can tell from the instructions, this recipe can be dangerous! Cooked sugar is approximately 380F (190°C). Do not make this recipe if you are distracted

PISTACHIO ICE CREAM

Makes about 2 pints (1 litre) of ice cream

¼ cup organic new-crop pistachios

1 tsp granulated sugar

2/3 cup heavy cream

2/3 cup whole milk

8 egg yolks

1/3 cup unpasteurized honey

¼ cup organic new-crop pistachios

1 tsp granulated sugar

This ice cream is inspired by Middle-Eastern frozen desserts. To take it to the next level, add a little rosewater

Coarsely grind the pistachios and sugar together with a mortar and pestle or in a small food processor. Set aside

Over medium heat in a heavy bottomed pot, warm the cream and milk together

In a separate bowl, whip the yolks and honey together until smooth, fluffy and lightened in colour

Whisk the hot cream mixture into the yolks a bit at a time until they are warmed

Whisk the warm yolk mixture back into the remaining hot cream in the pot

Cook over medium heat, stirring constantly until the mixture coats the back of a wooden spoon

Pass through a fine mesh strainer into a bowl set in an ice bath to stop the cooking process immediately. Add the pistachio mixture

Chill in the refrigerator at least 8 hours

Follow the instructions on your ice cream maker, removing the ice cream when it looks like a thick milkshake

Freeze at least 4 hours to allow the ice cream to set

Look for pistachios with bright green flesh. If they are brown or graying, they are old and will have lost their rich, buttery flavour. In this case, yes, organic really is best

SUGAR PUMPKIN CHEESECAKE

Makes eight individual cheesecakes

1 medium sized sugar pumpkin (2–3 lb)

1 lb cream cheese

¾ cups dark brown sugar

4 eggs

2 ½ tsp cinnamon

2 ½ tsp grated fresh ginger

¼ tsp ground nutmeg

¼ tsp ground ginger

This recipe calls for the use of a flexible silicone mold with at least eight individual size cavities. You can find them in specialty food stores, but if you don't have one on hand, you can substitute this filling for the one in any conventional cheesecake recipe and bake it in a 9-inch spring-form pan

Split the pumpkin in half and scoop out the seeds and strings. Rub a thin coat of canola or vegetable oil on the pumpkin skin and sprinkle the inside with cinnamon. Place the two halves cut-side-down on a baking sheet and roast them in a 350F (165°C) oven until the skin is browned and pulling away from the flesh (30–60 minutes depending on its size)

Peel the skin off the flesh and break it up into a colander. Allow the roasted pumpkin to drain until it has come to room temperature, then weigh the flesh to get 1 lb

Reduce the oven temperature to 200F (95°C)

In a mixer, using the paddle attachment, beat the cream cheese and sugar together until smooth

Add the eggs one at a time, scraping the sides of the bowl in between each addition

Add the roasted pumpkin and spices, mix until smooth

Spoon the mixture in to individual sized silicone molds

Bake for 1 hour

Allow the cheesecakes to chill completely in the refrigerator before turning out of the molds

If you wish, serve on gingerbread (p.111) crusts

Sugar pumpkins are quite small, are lower in moisture and have a more concentrated flavour than jack-o'-lanterns and other pumpkins. If you can't find them, you can use the big guys, but make sure you drain them really well

HOLIDAYS

As the year draws to a close, we celebrate the cycle of the seasons, the winter solstice and the new year with celebrations and traditions rooted in thankfulness, giving, sharing and family.

Cookies are baked and shared with friends and loved ones, feasts are prepared and liquor is often consumed.

In addition to being enjoyed as a libation, more booze makes its way into dessert at the holidays, perhaps because we allow ourselves a bit more license to indulge at this time of year.

Cranberries, one of the few fruits native to North America, are a traditional holiday flavour along with ginger and spices.

Fruitcake, the butt of many a joke, is equally enjoyed and loathed by all.

We choose colours to represent the season, including red and white, making red velvet cake (although delicious year-round), a particularly great choice as a festive dessert.

GINGERBOYS

Makes about 2 dozen cookies

Ingredients:
- 4 ¼ cups all-purpose flour
- 1 ½ cups dark brown sugar
- 4 tsp ground cinnamon
- 4 tsp ground ginger
- ½ tsp ground cloves
- ½ tsp kosher salt
- 2 Tbsp baking powder
- ½ lb cold cubed unsalted butter (2 sticks)
- 1 cup full-fat buttermilk
- 1/3 cup blackstrap molasses
- 2 Tbsp finely chopped candied ginger
- 2 tsp peeled and grated fresh ginger
- sugar for sprinkling

They don't have to be boys if you don't want them to be, but they'll always be soft, chewy, gingery and gone before you know it!

Pre-heat the oven to 350F (165°C)

In the bowl of a mixer, combine the flour, sugar, spices, salt and baking powder

Using the paddle attachment, cut in the cold butter until only pea-sized lumps remain

In a measuring cup or bowl, combine the buttermilk, molasses and gingers, then add them to the dry mixture

Mix until no dry spots remain

Roll out the dough on a lightly floured surface or between two pieces of parchment

Chill in the refrigerator until firm (at least 1 hour)

Cut the dough into boys or whatever shapes you desire, placing the cookies on a baking sheet at least 2 cm apart

Chill the dough in the freezer for at least 10 minutes

Sprinkle the boys' bellies with sugar just before they go in the oven

Bake until the bellies are puffed and the edges are golden brown (8–12 minutes)

Allow the cookies to cool on a rack for 10 minutes before eating them!

I love this recipe so much. So much

CRANBERRY CARDAMOM SHORTBREAD

Makes about 3 dozen cookies

Ingredients:
- ½ lb cold cubed unsalted butter (2 sticks)
- ¾ cups sifted icing sugar
- 1 2/3 cups all-purpose flour
- 2/3 cups rice flour
- ½ tsp ground cardamom
- 1 ½ tsp fresh lemon zest
- 1 tsp vanilla extract
- 1 egg
- 250g, dried organic cranberries

The rice flour produces a delicate crumbly texture by reducing the amount of gluten in the recipe

Pre-heat the oven to 350F (165°C)

In the bowl of a food processor, combine the butter, icing sugar, flour, rice flour and cardamom and process until smooth and homogenous

Add the lemon zest, vanilla and egg and continue processing until smooth

Turn out of the food processor and knead in the cranberries until they are evenly distributed

Roll the dough between two pieces of parchment or on a lightly floured surface until it is about 1/3 cm thick

Chill in the refrigerator until firm (at least 1 hour)

Cut the dough into whatever shapes you desire, placing the cookies on a baking sheet at least 2 cm apart

Chill the dough in the freezer for at least 10 minutes

Bake until the tops are firm and the edges are just turning golden brown (8–12 minutes)

Allow the cookies to cool on a rack for 10 minutes before eating them!

Dried cranberries are almost always sweetened, usually with glucose. Try to find ones with a lower sugar content, or ones sweetened with maple syrup or fruit juice concentrate, they'll deliver better flavour and nuance to these addictive cookies

VANILLA BEAN SUGAR COOKIES

Makes about 3 dozen cookies

1 ¼ cups softened unsalted butter (2½ sticks)

1 cup granulated sugar

1 egg

1 ½ tsp vanilla extract

pulp scraped from 1 whole vanilla bean (use the pod for vanilla syrup (p.140))

¼ tsp baking powder

3 cups all-purpose flour

sugar for sprinkling

Freezing the dough after rolling it makes the cookies easier to cut and improves their texture upon baking

Pre-heat the oven to 350F (165°C)

Cream the butter and sugar in a mixer using the paddle attachment until fluffy and light in colour

Add the egg, vanilla extract and pulp, scraping the sides of the bowl as necessary

Add the flour and baking powder and mix until combined

Turn out the dough onto a piece of plastic wrap and wrap it tightly. Flattening the dough will make it easier to work with

Chill in the refrigerator until firm (at least 1 hour)

Roll the dough between two pieces of parchment or on a lightly floured surface until it is about 1/3 cm thick

Chill the dough in the freezer for at least 10 minutes

Cut the dough into whatever shapes you desire, placing the cookies on a baking sheet at least 2 cm apart

Chill again before baking

Sprinkle the cookies with sugar

Bake until the tops are firm and the edges are just turning golden brown (8–12 minutes)

Allow the cookies to cool on a rack for 10 minutes before eating them!

Butter-based cookies are always best baked from frozen. Not only does it give them better texture, but it's utterly convenient. You can freeze the cookies on a baking sheet after rolling and cutting them, then keep them in a sealed plastic bag until you're ready to bake them!

NEWSCHOOL FRUITCAKE

Makes 1 9x12 inch pan

2&2/3 lb of different kinds of new-crop dried organic fruit (like peaches, pears, pineapple, apricots, cherries, currants, blueberries, cranberries, or whatever you desire) cut into equal sized chunks

½ cup bourbon

3 cups all-purpose flour

1 Tbsp baking soda

¾ tsp kosher salt

1 ¾ tsp fresh ground nutmeg

1 ¾ tsp ground ginger

1/8 tsp ground cinnamon

2/3 lb ground almonds

¾ cups crème fraiche or sour cream

6 Tbsp fresh squeezed lemon juice

4 Tbsp vanilla extract

¾ lb softened unsalted butter (3 sticks)

1 ½ cups granulated sugar

6 eggs

2 peeled and grated ripe pears

3 Tbsp chopped candied lemon or orange zest (p.145)

The opposite of oldschool, this fruitcake is made with dried fruit instead of candied, lots and lots of fresh nuts, and instead of soaking the cake in brandy, I soak my fruit in bourbon

Combine the dried fruit and bourbon in a sealed non-reactive container for a minimum of 24 hours (I like to soak my fruit, refrigerated, for six months to allow the flavours to really blend)

Pre-heat the oven to 275F (135°C)

In a large bowl, sift the flour, soda, salt, and spices together, then stir in the ground nuts until homogenous. Set aside

In a large measuring cup or bowl, combine the crème fraiche, lemon juice and vanilla extract until homogenous. Set aside

Cream the butter and sugar in a mixer using the paddle attachment until fluffy and light in colour

Add the eggs one at a time, scraping down the sides of the bowl with each addition

Add one third of the flour mixture and mix until combined

Add half the crème fraiche mixture and mix until combined, scraping the bowl as needed

Repeat the previous two steps: dry ingredients, then liquid, finishing with dry ingredients

Stir in the soaked fruit, nuts , grated pears and candied zest to distribute them all evenly through the batter

Spread the batter evenly into a greased or parchment lined pan

Bake for 1 hour, then turn the pan in the oven

continued...

Newschool Fruitcake Continued

Bake another 30 minutes, removing it from the oven once a thermometer inserted in the center reads 175F (80°C)

Allow the cake to cool 10 minutes before turning it out of the pan

Allow to cool to room temperature, then wrap the cake in a layer of parchment, followed by two layers of plastic wrap

Allow to rest in the refrigerator for at least a week before serving

This cake will keep, tightly wrapped in the refrigerator, for over a year. Its flavour will evolve over time

It's so important to use good ingredients for this recipe. Seek out the most beautiful fruit and nuts you can find, and let this recipe make them sing!

You can use any nuts in place of the ground almonds, and as usual, it's best if you grind them yourself in a food processor

ROASTED PUMPKIN TART

Enough for eight 4" tarts

1 small sugar pumpkin (1–2lb)

1 egg

½ cup heavy cream

¼ cup granulated sugar

3 Tbsp dark brown sugar

¾ tsp ground cinnamon

½ tsp fresh ginger, peeled and grated

¼ tsp freshly grated nutmeg

¼ tsp ground cloves

¼ tsp kosher salt

8 chilled, unbaked tart shells (p.135)

Chantilly cream (p.143)

dark maple syrup

This recipe can be made with canned pumpkin but it just won't be the same

Split the pumpkin in half and scoop out the seeds and strings. Rub a thin coat of canola or vegetable oil on the pumpkin's skin and sprinkle the inside with cinnamon. Place the two halves cut-side-down on a baking sheet and roast them in a 350F (165°C) oven until the skin is browned and pulling away from the flesh (30–60 minutes depending on their size)

Peel the skin off the flesh and break it up into a colander. Allow the roasted pumpkin to drain until it has come to room temperature, then weigh the flesh to get ½ lb

Combine the egg, cream, sugars, ginger, spices and salt with the drained pumpkin

Mix with a hand blender, hand-held mixer or potato masher until smooth and homogenous

Spoon the filling into the tart shells until they are nearly full

Bake 15 minutes, then turn and bake another 10 minutes until the filling is puffed and set

Allow to cool to room temperature, and garnish with Chantilly cream and maple syrup if desired

You won't believe the difference it makes when you use roasted pumpkin instead of the canned stuff. If you wind up cracking a can, however, seek out the best quality you can find, and make sure it's 100% pumpkin, not pumpkin pie filling

WILD CRANBERRY BUTTER TARTS

Enough for eight 4" tarts

1 egg

1 cup dark brown sugar

1 Tbsp white vinegar

¼ tsp vanilla extract

5 Tbsp melted unsalted butter

¼ tsp kosher salt

½ cup fresh or frozen wild cranberries (or substitute regular cranberries)

8 chilled, unbaked tart shells (p.135)

The tartness of the cranberries really balances out the sweetness of the brown sugar filling

Preheat the oven to 350F (165°C)

Mix the egg, brown sugar, vinegar, vanilla, butter and salt together until smooth and homogenous

Distribute the wild cranberries evenly between the eight tart shells placed on a baking sheet

Spoon the brown sugar filling over the cranberries to fill each shell about 2/3 full

Bake 20 minutes, then quickly and gently turn in the oven

Continue baking until the filling has puffed and browned right to the center. (another 10–15 minutes)

Serve at room temperature

Wild cranberries are smaller and more flavourful than their cultivated counterparts. They're hard to find, though, and I've made this recipe successfully with fresh cultivated cranberries from the farmer's market. Delicious!

EGG NOG ICE CREAM

Makes about 2 pints (1 litre) of ice cream

2/3 cup heavy cream

2/3 cup whole milk

¼ tsp freshly ground nutmeg

8 egg yolks

1/3 cup granulated sugar

1 oz dark rum

The base for this ice cream is also my recipe for egg nog the beverage. Make of that what you will

Over medium heat in a heavy bottomed pot, warm the cream and milk together with the nutmeg

In a separate bowl, whip the yolks and sugar together until smooth, fluffy and lightened in colour

Whisk the hot cream mixture into the yolks a bit at a time until they are warmed

Whisk the warm yolk mixture back into the remaining hot cream in the pot

Cook over medium heat, stirring constantly until the mixture coats the back of a wooden spoon

Pass through a fine mesh strainer into a bowl set in an ice bath to stop the cooking process immediately

Stir in the rum

Chill in the refrigerator at least 8 hours

Follow the instructions on your ice cream maker, removing the ice cream when it looks like a thick milkshake

Freeze at least 4 hours to allow the ice cream to set

Ho ho ho

Grating the nutmeg fresh will make all the difference. There are special nutmeg grating tools, but you can use a rasp or the spiky side of a box grater. Just mind your fingers!

GINGER ICE CREAM

Makes about 2 pints (1 litre) of ice cream

2/3 cup heavy cream
2/3 cup whole milk
3 Tbsp grated fresh ginger
pinch ground ginger
8 egg yolks
1/3 cup granulated sugar
1 Tbsp finely diced candied ginger

This spicy ice cream is a favourite of mine with apple desserts

Over medium heat in a heavy bottomed pot, warm the cream and milk together with the grated and ground ginger

In a separate bowl, whip the yolks and sugar together until smooth, fluffy and lightened in colour

Whisk the hot cream mixture into the yolks a bit at a time until they are warmed

Whisk the warm yolk mixture back into the remaining hot cream in the pot

Cook over medium heat, stirring constantly until the mixture coats the back of a wooden spoon

Pass through a fine mesh strainer into a bowl set in an ice bath to stop the cooking process immediately

Chill in the refrigerator at least 8 hours

Follow the instructions on your ice cream maker, removing the ice cream when it looks like a thick milkshake

Just before removing from the ice cream machine, add the candied ginger and process a few seconds to allow it to mix in

Freeze at least 4 hours to allow the ice cream to set

When you shred the ginger, don't worry too much about peeling it. Worry more about getting all the delicious spicy ginger juice into the milk. Don't leave it behind in the grater or on the counter!

RED VELVET CAKE WITH VANILLA BEAN FROSTING
Makes a 4-layer 7" cake

RED VELVET CAKE

¼ cup unsalted butter (½ a stick)

1 ½ cups granulated sugar

2 eggs

2 Tbsp red liqua-gel food colouring (see note below)

2 Tbsp water

2 Tbsp sifted cocoa

1 tsp Mexican vanilla extract

3 cups cake flour, measured then sifted

1 tsp kosher salt

1 cup full-fat buttermilk

1 tsp apple cider vinegar

1 tsp baking soda

This cake harkens back to the time before "Dutch process cocoa", when raw cocoa lent all chocolate cakes a bit of a reddish hue. Someone, somewhere decided to add some red food colouring to their chocolate cake to give it a more "traditional" look, then dropped the whole bottle in and red velvet cake was born!

One mustn't forget that in addition to being red, this cake is also called "velvet", a texture achieved by the old-fashioned leavening produced by baking soda and vinegar. Without this step, it's just chocolate cake with food colouring

CAKE

Pre-heat the oven to 350F (165°C)

Grease two 7" straight-sided cake pans and line the bottoms with parchment rounds

In a mixer, using the paddle attachment, beat the butter and sugar together until fluffy and lightened in colour

Add the eggs one at a time, scraping the sides of the bowl in between each addition

In a small, separate bowl, whisk together the food colouring, cocoa and vanilla to make a paste

Add the cocoa mixture to the batter, mixing until the colour is uniform, scraping down the sides and bottom of the bowl as needed

In the same small bowl, combine the salt and buttermilk, mopping up any of the red mixture still clinging to the sides of the bowl. Set aside

continued...

If you use a grocery-store food colouring, omit the water and increase the amount to ¼ cup. I've never had success with either powdered or natural food colourings

Red Velvet Cake Continued

Add 1/3 of the sifted flour to the batter and mix it in

Once the batter is homogenous, add ½ of the buttermilk mixture, mixing, once again until the batter is smooth

Repeat the above two steps, then add the last 1/3 of the flour mixture to the batter

Using a rubber spatula, make sure the batter is thoroughly mixed

In a fresh small bowl, combine the vinegar and baking soda, then quickly and thoroughly mix the foaming mixture into the batter with the rubber spatula

Immediately divide the batter between the two pans

Bake on the center rack of the oven for 20 minutes, then quickly and gently turn them around

Continue baking until a probe inserted in the center comes out clean (another 10–20 minutes)

Allow the cakes to rest 10 minutes before turning them out of the pan and setting them on cooling racks

Do not cut the cakes until they have completely cooled to room temperature!

This is real-deal old-fashioned Red Velvet Cake. I've never tasted a better recipe, and unlike most red velvet cakes, it doesn't taste strongly of food colouring. Change anything about the mixing method, and it just doesn't turn out the same. You've been warned!

Red Velvet Cake Continued

<u>VANILLA BEAN FROSTING</u>

1 cup whole milk

¼ vanilla bean

3 Tbsp all-purpose flour

½ lb room temperature unsalted butter (2 sticks)

1 cup granulated sugar

¾ tsp pure vanilla extract

There's a lot of debate about the right frosting to go with red velvet cake, and although there are those who swear by cream cheese, I swear by this stuff, so there!

FROSTING

Measure the milk and salt into a small, heavy bottomed saucepan

Whisk the flour into the milk and cook over medium heat, whisking constantly until the mixture bubbles and thickens

Measure the milk into a small, heavy bottomed saucepan

Slit open the vanilla bean and scrape out the seeds into the milk. Add the scraped pod

Remove from the heat and cover the surface with parchment or plastic wrap so that it doesn't develop a skin

Allow the milk mixture to cool to hand temperature. Remove the vanilla pod

In the bowl of a mixer using the whisk attachment, beat the butter until creamy

Gradually add the sugar, beating until fluffy and lightened in colour

Add the vanilla extract and beat well

Add the milk mixture and beat until smooth. If the mixture is too warm, it will look thin and soupy, if it is too cold, it will look curdled

If it is too warm, chill it in the refrigerator for 10 minutes and beat it again

If it is too cold, just keep beating it, and eventually it will become smooth, fluffy, and noticeably whiter

It is impossible to ruin this frosting. It will ALWAYS come together at the right temperature. Don't despair, it's worth the effort!

Red Velvet Cake Continued

ASSEMBLY

Using a serrated slicer, level the tops of each cake, then split each cake into two equal layers

Spread a layer of vanilla bean frosting over the bottom layer of cake, then top it with another layer of cake, repeating until you have a four-layer cake

Spread a thin layer of frosting on the outside of the cake and chill until the frosting is firm

Coat the cake in a thicker layer of frosting, smoothing out any uneven areas and leveling the top if required

If desired, pipe decorations on the top or sides of the cake, or decorate it with fresh seasonal fruit

This cake is best if allowed to sit for 6–24 hours after being assembled. Make it a day ahead for best results. While you wait for it, you can munch on cake tops and leftover frosting!

RED VELVET RUM BALLS

Makes about 3 dozen balls

Ingredients:
- 1 cup pecan pieces
- 4 cups of crumbled red velvet cake (p.127)
- 1 cup icing sugar
- 1 Tbsp cocoa powder
- ½ tsp kosher salt
- 3 oz dark rum
- 1/3 cup dark cane syrup
- icing sugar, cocoa powder or melted chocolate for dipping

This is a great use for leftover red velvet cake tops. Throw them in a sealed plastic bag in the freezer after trimming them from your cakes (if you can resist eating them!)

Oh, and (obviously) these are not for children

Pre-heat the oven to 350F (165°C)

Place the pecans on a baking sheet and roast them in the oven until they are aromatic and lightly browned (3–6 minutes).

Finely chop the warm pecans, or pulse them in a food processor

Combine the nuts with the red velvet crumbs, the sift in the icing sugar, cocoa and salt

Add the rum and syrup and mix with your hands or a wooden spoon until no dry spots remain (the mixture will be quite wet)

Allow the rum to absorb for at least 8 hours

Roll the mixture into 1-inch balls

Chill in the refrigerator until firm (at least 1 hour)

Dust with icing sugar or cocoa

Store in an airtight container in the refrigerator up to three months

For extra love, you can dip these in chocolate to turn them into red velvet cake truffles.

Feel free to skip the pecans or substitute them for a different nut if you wish

BASE RECIPES

VANILLA TART SHELLS

Makes about 16 4" tart shells

3 1/3 cups all-purpose flour

¼ tsp kosher salt

½ lb cold cubed unsalted butter (2 sticks)

3 cups icing sugar, measured then sifted

2 eggs

1 tsp vanilla extract

This dough is amazing in its patching ability. If it tears a little, you can "glue" it back together just by pressing it gently

Sift the flour and salt together into the bowl of a mixer

Add the cold butter, and blend with the paddle attachment on low speed until the mixture is sandy in texture

In a separate bowl, combine the icing sugar, eggs and vanilla extract to form a thick paste

Add the paste to the flour mixture and mix on low speed until combined

Turn out the dough onto a piece of plastic wrap and wrap it tightly. Flattening the dough will make it easier to work with

Chill in the refrigerator until firm (at least 1 hour)

Roll the dough on a lightly floured surface until it is about 1/3 cm thick

Cut about circles about 6" around draping each one inside a tart pan or ring

Gently tuck the dough into the corners of the mold, then trim any excess dough hanging off the top of the pan

Chill in the freezer at least 10 minutes before baking

continued…

I settled on this recipe years ago after trying dozens of different ones. It offers the crumbly buttery texture I love along with enough stability to be used in retail operations. Now it's yours!

You can re-roll the scraps once, but after that, discard them. The gluten gets over-processed and the tarts become tough

Vanilla Tart Shells Continued

FOR UNBAKED SHELLS

Store the unbaked shells in their pans, sealed in an airtight plastic bag in the freezer until they are needed

Do not defrost, and use as directed

FOR PARBAKED SHELLS

Pre-heat the oven to 350F (165°C)

Line each chilled tart shell with a piece of parchment large enough to cover the entire base and sides of the shell

Pour uncooked beans or rice on top of the parchment to weigh down the shells

Bake until the edges of the shells are golden brown and pulling away from the sides of their pans

Allow to cool to room temperature before using

FOR CHOCOLATE SHELLS

Substitute 3 cups of flour and 1/3 cup of sifted cocoa powder for the flour in the recipe

Always take the time to weight the parbaked tart shells. Not only does it help them keep their shape, but it prevents the inside from browning, making it a more receptive surface for bonding with a filling. Whenever I skip this step, I scold myself afterward

WHITE CHOCOLATE MOUSSE

Makes about 5 cups

½ lb good-quality white chocolate (like Valrhôna Ivoire)

¼ cup unsalted butter (½ a stick)

¼ cup vanilla bean custard (p.142)

1 egg white

3 cups heavy cream

This versatile mousse is both flavoured and stabilized by the white chocolate.

In a stainless steel bowl, melt the chocolate and butter together over a pot of simmering water

Add the custard and egg whites and mix with a heavy whisk until combined

In the bowl of a mixer, whip the cream to soft peaks

Stir 1/3 of the whipped cream into the chocolate mixture until smooth and homogenous

Gently fold the rest of the cream into the mousse

Chill undisturbed in the refrigerator for at least 4 hours before using

Store in the refrigerator up to 1 week

White chocolate is the most expensive chocolate due to its high cocoa butter content. The more expensive the white chocolate you purchase, the higher the cocoa butter percentage, and the more neutral it will taste

HOMEMADE MASCARPONE

Makes about 2 cups

4 cups heavy cream
1 tsp tartaric acid
¼ tsp icing sugar

Good mascarpone can be hard to find. When in doubt, make your own!

Using a thermometer, warm the cream to 140F (60°C) over medium-low heat

Whisk in the tartaric acid and sugar

Whisking constantly, heat the cream to 180F (82°C)

Remove the cream from the heat and allow to cool to room temperature

Line a strainer with three damp coffee filters, and place the strainer over a bowl or pot

Pour the cream into the lined strainer and cover the strainer with plastic wrap

Put the entire apparatus in the refrigerator and allow it to drain undisturbed for 24 hours

Remove the mascarpone from the strainer and use immediately or store in the refrigerator up to 5 days

Tartaric acid can be found in health-food stores and some pharmacies. You only need to be careful with it in its granular form, avoid contact with your eyes and nasal passages

VANILLA BEAN SYRUP

Makes approximately 4 cups (1 litre)

3 cups granulated sugar

1 cup boiling water

Scraped vanilla bean pods

This versatile sweetener can add a kick to just about anything, my favorite being a morning latte

Pour the boiling water over the sugar and stir until the sugar is completely dissolved

Place any unused vanilla pods you have left over from a recipe that called for the seeds but not the pod into a squeeze bottle or jar

Pour the hot syrup over the vanilla pods and allow the mixture to infuse at least 24 hours

Store at room temperature

Feel free to add more vanilla beans as you acquire them and pour fresh hot syrup overtop as you use it up

Great for sweetening fruit that may be a bit underripe, adding a light glaze or just to give a little je-ne-sais-quoi to your desserts, this stuff is great to keep around and a wonderful use for vanilla beans gone astray

VANILLA BEAN CUSTARD

Makes about 3 cups

2/3 cup heavy cream

2/3 cup whole milk

1/3 vanilla bean, scraped

8 egg yolks

1/3 cup granulated sugar

½ tsp vanilla extract

If you want vanilla ice cream, process this recipe in your ice cream machine according to the manufacturer's instructions. You're welcome!

Over medium heat in a heavy bottomed pot, warm the cream, milk and vanilla bean together

In a separate bowl, whip the yolks and sugar together until smooth, fluffy and lightened in colour

Whisk the hot cream mixture into the yolks a bit at a time until they are warmed

Whisk the warm yolk mixture back into the remaining hot cream in the pot

Cook over medium heat, stirring constantly until the mixture coats the back of a wooden spoon

Pass through a fine mesh strainer into a bowl set in an ice bath to stop the cooking process immediately

Stir in the vanilla extract

Store in the refrigerator up to 1 week

The best vanilla I've ever sourced comes from The Vanilla Company based out of Santa Cruz, California. Their vanilla beans and extract are second to none, the Paplanta Mexican extract being my all-time favourite

CHANTILLY CREAM

Makes approximately 4 cups (1 litre)

2 cups cold heavy cream

1 ½ tsp icing sugar

seeds from ½ a vanilla bean

Chantilly cream is a fancy name for whipped cream with vanilla bean. Now you can make everything sound fancier!

Whip the cream until it forms soft peaks

Add the icing sugar and vanilla seeds (the stuff you scrape out from inside the bean)

Whip a little more until the peaks are just firm

Use immediately

If you don't have a vanilla bean, use ¼ tsp of good vanilla extract. Alternately, there are some good vanilla powder or vanilla paste products on the market, feel free to use them as well. That being said, there's nothing to rival the flavour of freshly scraped vanilla bean!

CANDIED LEMON ZEST

Fresh lemon peel, cut with a channel knife into thick strands

Granulated sugar

Many people claim not to like candied peel, but I think it's because they've never tried a really good example. Often, manufacturers don't blanch the peel enough times to eliminate the bitterness.

Cover the lemon peels with fresh, cold water in a pot large enough to hold them

Bring the water to a boil over maximum heat

As soon as the water has boiled, dump the peels into a strainer, and run cold water over them

Return them to their pot and repeat the above three steps at least four more times

Taste the boiled peel to see if it still tastes bitter. If it does, repeat the blanching process again, tasting after each time until no bitterness remains.

Drain the peels, return them to their pot and cover them with sugar

Add enough water to moisten all the sugar, then place over medium-low heat

Allow the sugar to dissolve without stirring, then simmer the peels in the heavy syrup until they are sweet and translucent

Spread a 1cm thick layer of sugar on a tray or baking sheet

Strain the peels and spread them out on the dry sugar, then bury them in more sugar and allow them to dry out at room temperature for 24 hours

Remove the peels from the sugar and store, refrigerated in an airtight container up to 3 months

You can use the lemon syrup more than once, and the sugar tastes great in lemonade.
This recipe can be used with any citrus fruit, grapefruit and blood oranges making particularly lovely candies. I can't say I care for the taste of candied lime zest, though, it's incurably bitter

SOURCES

Golda's Kitchen
www.goldaskitchen.com
For Canadian customers, there's no better selection or prices than this Ontario-based online kitchen equipment store.

JB Prince
www.jbprince.com
Based out of New York City, JB Prince is the main importer of specialty culinary tools for North America. If you can't find it anywhere, you can find it a JB Prince. Their online ordering is easy, and shipment to Canada via UPS is less than 48 hours.

New England Cheesemaking Company
www.cheesemaking.com
The New England Cheesemaking Company has been preaching the gospel of home-cheesemaking for well over a decade. The cultures ship in little packets, and deliver in 1–2 weeks.

Rancho Vignola
www.ranchovignola.com
Whenever I talk about new-crop dried fruit and nuts in this book, I'm talking about products from Rancho Vignola. This company spends half the year sourcing the highest quality ingredients, spends the fall drying them out, and the winter selling them. They only sell once a year, so stock up in early November.

The Vanilla Company
www.vanilla.com
Visit the Vanilla Queen's domain and learn about quality, ethical vanilla production from around the globe. Then purchase some of her second-to-none vanilla beans, extracts, pastes and powders. One caution, when these products go through customs, they get some rough handling, be prepared to accept some punctured bags or leaking if your order is being shipped to Canada.

INDEX

APPLE
Pudding Cake p91
Roasted Chestnut Tart p99

BERRY
BlackB & Passionfruit
Mousse Tart p70
B Conserve p75
Key Lime & BlueB Tart p76
Lemon Chiffon & B Cake p58
Summer B Sorbet p79
Triple RaspB Tart p83

BUTTERMILK
Blood Orange Tart p22
Ice Cream p53

CAKE
Apple Pudding p91
Carrot Chiffon p34
Lemon Chiffon p58
Newschool Fruitcake p117
Red Velvet p127

CARAMEL
Fleur-de-Sel Ice Cream p40
Walnut & Rosemary Tart p31
Whisky Sauce p102

CARROT
Chiffon Cake p34

CHANTILLY CREAM p143

CHEESE
Blue Ice Cream p86
Cake, Cherry Tart p80
Cake, Fromage Blanc p49
Cake, Sugar Pumpkin p105
Mascarpone, Homemade p139

CHEESECAKE
Cherry Tart p80
Fromage Blanc p49
Sugar Pumpkin p105

CHERRY
Cheesecake Tart p80
Sour Crumble Tart p95

CHOCOLATE
Tart Shells p137
White Mousse p138

COBBLER
Peach p72

COMPOTE
Damson Plum p97

CONSERVE
Berry p75

COOKIES
Cranberry Cardamom p112
Gingerboys p111
Hazelnut Baci p25
Lemon Lav. Shortbread p50
Oatmeal Raisin p96
Rum & Raisin Roundies p57
Vanilla Bean Sugar p115

CORN
Sweet Ice Cream p92

CRANBERRY
Cardamom Shortbread p112
Wild Butter Tarts p123

CURD
Fragrant Lemon p54
Key Lime p76
Passionfruit p46

FIG
Honey Mousse Tart p84

FOOL
Punk Rock Rhubarb p45

FROSTING
Lemon p61
Maple p37
Vanilla Bean p129

FRUITCAKE
Newschool p117

GINGER
Boys p111
Ice Cream p125

HONEY
Ice Cream p69
Fig Mousse Tart p84
Tangerine Sorbet p32

ICE CREAM
Blue Cheese p86
Buttermilk p53
Egg Nog p124
Fleur-de-Sel Caramel p40
Ginger p125
Honey p69
Pistachio p103
Single Malt Scotch p21
Sweet Corn p92
Vanilla Bean p142

KEY LIME
Blueberry Tart p76
Curd p76

LEMON
Candied Zest p145
Chiffon Cake p58
Fragrant Tart p54
Frosting p61
Lavender Shortbread p50
Mousse p62

MANGO
Passionfruit Tart p46

MAPLE
Frosting p37

MOUSSE
Honey p84
Lemon p62
Mascarpone p80
Passionfruit p70
White Chocolate p138

NUTS
Hazelnut Baci p25
Keegan's Spiced p27
Pistachio Ice Cream p103
R. Apple & Chestnut Tart p99
Sweet Potato Pecan Tart p28

Walnut & Rosem. Cml. Tart p31

OAT
Crumble Topping p95
Meal Cookies p96

ORANGE
Blood O & Buttermilk Tart p22
Honey Tangerine Sorbet p32

PASSIONFRUIT
Blackberry Mousse Tart p70
Mango Tart p46

PEACH
Cobbler p72

PLUM
Damson Compote p97

PUDDING
Apple Cake p91
Sticky Toffee p100

PUMPKIN
Roasted Tart p120
Sugar Cheesecake p105

RAISIN
Oatmeal Cookies p96
Rum Roundies p57

RASPBERRY
Triple Tart p83

RED VELVET
Cake p127
Rum Balls p132

RHUBARB
Punk Rock Fool p45

RUM
Egg Nog Ice Cream p124
Raisin Roundies p57
Red Velvet Balls p132

SCOTCH
Single Malt Ice Cream p21

SHORTBREAD
Cranberry Cardamom p112
Lemon Lavender p50

SORBET
Honey Tangerine p32
Summer Berry p79

TARTS
Blood Orange & Buttermilk p22
Blackbry & Pssfrt Mousse p70
Cherry Cheesecake p80
Chocolate Shells p137
Fig & Honey Mousse p84
Fragrant Lemon p54
Key Lime & Blueberry p76
Passionfruit & Mango p46
Roasted Apple & Chestnut p99
Roasted Sugar Pumpkin p105
Sour Cherry Crumble p95
Sweet Potato Pecan p28
Triple Raspberry p83
Vanilla Shells p135
Walnut & Rsmry Caramel p31
Wild Cranberry Butter p123

VANILLA BEAN
Chantilly Cream p143
Custard p142
Frosting p129
Ice Cream p142
Sugar Cookies p115
Syrup p140
Tart Shells p135

WHISKY
Single Malt Ice Cream p21
Caramel Sauce p102

ABOUT THE AUTHOR

Rebekah started studying the culinary arts after realizing that her love of hospitality greatly outweighed her desire work 9 to 5.

She learned to bake as part of her studies in professional cooking, and by the time she completed her culinary apprenticeship, she had become better at making desserts than anyone she knew, and decided to make sweets her full-time gig.

She created Nectar Desserts, a popular dessert bar, patisserie and catering company in 2006. Her favorite dessert is crème caramel, which she rarely makes because she winds up eating it all.

Aside from dessert, her interests include wine, education, business and comic books. She currently divides her time between travelling, working as a hospitality consultant, and writing.

"I did not ordinar
uat, plump little
scallop shell. And
a spoonful of the
hed my palate than
quisite pleasure had i
s of life had becom
which love has of fi
Whence could it
t it infinitely transc
apprehend it?

Made in the USA
Charleston, SC
23 May 2011